ROSYTH:
GARDEN CITY
&
ROYAL DOCKYARD

Rosyth Garden City
Millennium Project

Edited by
Leonie Chalkley and Margaret Shiach

Printed by Fife Council Print Services, Scotland

Published by Rosyth Garden City Millennium Project

Edited by Leonie Chalkley and Margaret Shiach

Printed by Fife Council Print Services, Scotland

Back Cover Photographs

Queensferry Road, Rosyth, circa 1920
and
Arrival of HMS Ark Royal at Rosyth Royal Dockyard for refit in 1999

Acknowledgements

This book was partly funded by the Royal Incorporation of Architects in Scotland Millennium Awards.

Millennium Awards

We are grateful to the following bodies and individuals who have kindly given permission to reproduce photographs and drawings in this book:

Babcock Engineering Services, Rosyth
Dunfermline Carnegie Library - Local History Collection
Imperial War Museum, London
Innovation, Rosyth
Inverkeithing Local History Society
J7 Digital Photography, Rosyth
Lauder College, Dunfermline
Lexmark International (Scotland)

London School of Economics
First Garden City Heritage Museum, Letchworth
Royal Commission on the Ancient & Historic Monuments of Scotland
Lena Morris
Martin Rogers
Margaret Shiach
William Hutchinson

We are also grateful to Irene May and Frank Pope who have given permission for some of their childhood memories to be incorporated in this book.

Paper for this book was kindly donated by Tullis Russell Papermakers - www.trg.co.uk

Printed on Mellotex Brilliant White 250 & 160 gsm produced by Tullis Russell Papermakers

i

Table of Contents

Contents

Foreword

Rt. Hon. Gordon Brown MP

Every community has its own story to tell and Rosyth has an exceptional story which is told in this book.

For the town of Rosyth has a unique place in Scotland's history. It is Scotland's Garden City. Its dockyard was the first and premier naval dockyard in Scotland. Its Naval Base has had an important role in supporting the Royal Navy in two world wars and after.

When Councillor Pat Callaghan asked me to write an introduction I was delighted to do so to congratulate the members of the group who have produced this book. Through the pages of this book we are reminded of our heritage and learn how the dockyard came into being and its role during the Great War; how Rosyth came to be built as a Garden City and the background to the Garden City movement; the role

of the dockyard during the Second World War and how the war affected the civilian population; the changes which took place in Rosyth and the dockyard in two decades - the 1950s and 1980s when I was honoured to become MP for Rosyth and surrounding areas; and the recent changes as the town and dockyard face up to the new challenges and opportunities in the 21st Century.

The illustrated account along with memories of some of the people who have lived in Rosyth remind us of what life was like in a dockyard town both in times of war and of peace. I am sure the book will awaken memories among those who have lived in Rosyth for many years. For others it will give an insight into the ups and downs which the town and dockyard have experienced over the years.

It shows us that Rosyth is a community which has had to endure the tragedies of war, the adversities of recession and yet has emerged stronger - a community from which people can travel thousands of miles around the world but still think of Rosyth as home. It is a community which has always taken a pride in its young people and has had a special place for its old folk who have served the community all their lives. I am privileged to know Rosyth and to be a neighbour down the road. Whether you are a long-time resident of Rosyth or a newcomer, I very much hope you will enjoy reading Rosyth's story.

Introduction

Margaret Shiach

Members of the Rosyth Garden City Millennium Project
Back Row: Sandy Masterton, Alasdair Macmillan and Martin Rogers
Front Row: Bunty Paterson, Margaret Shiach and Pat Callaghan
Not pictured: Felicity Greenfields and Leonie Chalkley

The group writing this book formed because we felt that Rosyth had a unique claim on Scotland's history. The fortunes of Rosyth Dockyard and its Garden City have been closely linked over the years. Therefore, we felt it only right that their stories should be told. It is the group's ambition to share with local people, and a wider audience, something of Rosyth's architectural and naval history in the hope that this architectural 'fragmentation' can be turned around and its heritage preserved. As a group we have become like Rosyth itself - a community diverse in talents and strengths. The balance of the team bringing together the history of the area (Martin Rogers, Felicity Greenfields, Pat Callaghan, and Margaret Shiach), the history of the community (Sandy Masterton and Bunty Paterson), editing, web production and CD-Rom creation (Leonie Chalkley and Alasdair Macmillan) have created a merging of our backgrounds, a forming of new friendships and partnerships, just like Rosyth itself. Rosyth's legacy of community spirit in helping your neighbour, its diversity of opinion, talents and strengths all blended to form a positive drive forward. We hope to produce a tangible resource that can be passed on to future generations as it is through Rosyth's children that Rosyth will develop its true potential. We hope that Rosyth's children will know and be proud of their heritage and that no child will again be heard to say "Who built that castle in the middle of an industrial site? That's daft!"

Our hope for the future is that Rosyth will be recognised as a major part of Scotland's and the UK's heritage. We also hope that Rosyth be given the credit it deserves as a world heritage site of architectural vision, community vision and as an embracer of new strategies to keep Rosyth a strong and key player in the world of industry.

The Early Days of the Dockyard

Martin Rogers

It was quite a common sight to see ships of the Royal Navy in the River Forth in the 19th and early 20th Centuries. The Forth provided a natural anchorage and it was a useful stopping off place for ships on their way to and from exercises in the northern waters of Britain. When the Government were looking for a site for a new Naval Base on the east coast of Britain, the bay of St. Margaret's Hope was chosen.

Rosyth Castle in 1911 as the Dockyard construction work proceeded. The railway line into the site can be seen in the foreground. (Dunfermline Carnegie Library)

Standing on a rocky outcrop within the site was Rosyth Castle. This had been built at the end of the 15th Century as part of the Barony of Rosyth which was then held by a branch of the Stewart family. About 100 yards north of the castle stood the castle doocot built to provide

1

shelter for doos (pigeons). Rosyth Castle's doocot is not quite as old as the castle, dating from the 16th Century, and has 1500 nesting boxes. The pigeons and their eggs were used as a ready source of food, particularly in the winter months. Although the doocot has remained in a very good state of repair, the castle itself became uninhabited in the early 18th Century and gradually lapsed into a ruinous state. Many of the stones from the buildings round the castle would have been re-cycled to build and repair other buildings in the neighbourhood.

Site of an accident to Frank Frail in July 1914. He fell off the staging, fractured his skull and died later in hospital. (Dunfermline Carnegie Library)

The decision to build the Naval Base at St. Margaret's Hope was announced in 1903 but it was some years before work began. In the interim period, a railway line was constructed into the site (completed in 1907) and a new road (Admiralty Road) was built from the outskirts of Inverkeithing through to near Pattiesmuir (completed 1909). Later in 1909 the main contract for building the Dockyard was let to the firm of Easton Gibb & Son. This was an enormous undertaking requiring the excavation of tons of soil, mud and rock for the docks and basins. The construction of the main (non-tidal) basin was particularly difficult as large concrete blocks (monoliths) had to be sunk on top of each other to form the basin walls. The Forth Bridge, another major civil engineering project completed some 20 years previously, dominates the landscape and people still marvel at that feat of engineering. The Dockyard works on the other hand, are largely unseen and it is difficult now to appreciate the scale and complexity of the project. Working conditions were very primitive and, surprising as it may seem, there were more men killed (in excess of 60) in building the Dockyard than were killed during the building of the Forth Bridge. Most of the men employed on the construction work were navvies (labourers) and came from many different parts of the United Kingdom to work on the contract. At its peak there were about 5000 men employed on building the Dockyard and the plant included 30 locomotives, 900 wagons, 12 concrete mixers, 90 steam and 24 electric cranes.

There was no town of Rosyth in the early days of the building of the Dockyard and the navvies had to find lodgings in the surrounding area - Inverkeithing, Charlestown and Dunfermline. A number of model lodging houses were built to accommodate the men. The present day Comfort Store at Jamestown, Inverkeithing, was the largest one built. It was called the Naval Base Mansions and was opened in June 1910 with room for 660 men. In order to provide some local housing, Easton Gibb brought up some second hand corrugated iron huts which had been used by the Great Central Railway Company during the construction of the Immingham Docks. These were erected in 1913 accommodating 1000 men. Families lived in part of the huts with from four to 26 lodgers living in the other part. A second batch of new huts was built the following year on land to the east. These were smaller and of better quality and were mostly intended for families. This community was known as Tin Town or, more grandly, Bungalow City. The huts were built on the north side of Hilton Road roughly where Brankholm Lane, Cunningham Road, Tovey Road and McGrigor Road are today. A Navvy Mission had been set up to provide for the spiritual needs of the men, initially with bases in Inverkeithing and Charlestown. When the Tin Town was built, a corrugated iron Church was also provided which became the main centre of the Navvy Mission. A large number of social activities were organised for the inhabitants. There were no fewer than four football teams, a rugby team and a cricket team in operation and tennis courts and a miniature rifle range. Picture shows were given in the village hall. A Social Council was set up to act as something like a village parliament with Easton Gibb, the east village and the west village each nominating six members.

Work under way in July 1914 on erecting the second phase of Tin Town. The original Tin Town settlement and Rosyth Cottages can be seen in the left centre of the photo. (Dunfermline Carnegie Library)

Work on the Dockyard progressed steadily. It attracted much interest and over the years there were many visitors to the site to see the work taking place. These included engineering students, members of Dunfermline Town Council, Herbert Asquith (Prime Minister), Winston Churchill (the First Lord of the Admiralty), Crown Prince Hirohito of

DUNFERMLINE FATHERS INVADING ROSYTH.

Transplanted from "the wild and woolly West" to Rosyth, the car in which Colonel Cody used to tour is to carry Dunfermline Town Councillors round the Government works next Wednesday. Our cartoonist has tried to depict the "exciting" scene.

A cartoon from the People's Journal depicting a visit to the Dockyard by members of Dunfermline Town Council in August 1910.

This photo taken in 1913 gives some idea of the amount of work required to excavate and construct the graving docks. This is Dock No. 1 which can be divided into two sections by means of a floating caisson. (Dunfermline Carnegie Library)

Japan, the King and Queen of Belgium, King George V and Queen Mary, Josephus Daniels (the US Naval Secretary) and the Shah of Persia. There were so many visitors that Easton Gibb bought a railway carriage to take visitors round the site. The carriage had formerly been owned by Buffalo Bill when he toured in this country with his Wild West Show.

As the work progressed, the Admiralty extended the contract to provide for three docks instead of one and to require a greater depth of water in the submarine basin. This delayed the completion of the contract and when the Great War started in 1914 the Dockyard was not ready to dock or repair ships. Many of the men working in the Dockyard enlisted in the army or navy and there were real fears that it would not be possible to complete the building of the Dockyard. However the decision was taken to press ahead with the work and, with the help of sailors from the

Grand Fleet, the Dockyard became operational in March 1916. This was not a moment too soon because the greatest naval battle of the War (the Battle of Jutland) took place on 31 May 1916 during which a number of ships were sunk or badly damaged. The Dockyard was soon busy repairing many of these ships including HMS Lion (Admiral Beatty's

The battleship HMS Warspite of the Queen Elizabeth super dreadnought class in dry dock at Rosyth after the Battle of Jutland in 1916. (Dunfermline Carnegie Library)

6

flagship), HMS Tiger, HMS Southampton, HMS Warspite and HMS Princess Royal. It has been calculated that during the war the Dockyard repaired and refitted 78 capital ships, 82 light cruisers and 37 smaller craft.

The No. 34 tram waiting at the tram terminus in Hilton Road (opposite the present day sub-post office). The Tin Town huts can be seen in the background. The photo dates from about 1920.
(Dunfermline Carnegie Library)

To help transport workmen to the Dockyard, tram lines were laid from Dunfermline to Rosyth in 1917. They ran down the middle of the dual carriageway between Dunfermline and Rosyth, then across fields (along the line of what was to become King's Road) and down the west side of Castle Road to the terminus in Hilton Road. Other workmen who lived in Edinburgh travelled to work by train. In 1918 there were no fewer than four workmen's trains between Edinburgh and the Dockyard railway station carrying over 4000 men daily to and from their various shifts.

The war ended with the signing of the Armistice on 11 November 1918. The German Navy was required to surrender the bulk of their

Fleet to the Royal Navy and the surrender of 74 surface warships took place in the Firth of Forth on 21 November 1918. The 14 squadrons of the Grand Fleet formed up in two columns and went out to meet the German ships to the west of May Island. The German Fleet than had to pass between the two columns on the way to its anchorage off Inchkeith Island. Later the German ships were escorted to Scapa Flow in Orkney where they were interned. However, that is not the end of the story. The German ships feature in Rosyth Dockyard's story some years later.

The main Naval Stores storehouse nearing completion in 1922. Popularly known as Alcatraz it was demolished in 1998. (Dunfermline Carnegie Library)

In February 1918, Easton Gibb's contract was taken over by the Admiralty and many of Easton Gibb's employees transferred to the Admiralty. Although the hourly rate paid by the Admiralty was less, the weekly earnings were better taking into account war bonuses and overtime rates over the standard working week of 48 hours. Weekly earnings for a labourer working a 56 ½ hour week would be about £3 0s 7d (i.e. £3.03p). After the completion of the contract works, storehouses were built and work proceeded on extending the North Wall. At the time it was intended that the North Wall would stretch for some 3000 feet with a breakwater parallel to it some 4500 feet long creating a second tidal basin or harbour. This was never completed.

Initial plans for the Dockyard made provision for a coal handling yard but in about 1910, the Admiralty decided to move to oil rather then coal as the principal fuel for Royal Naval ships. In 1914, work began on the construction of a huge concrete oil fuel reservoir on the site of the former sandstone quarry at Howe Cove. This was completed in 1919 and had a capacity of 250,000 tons (60 million gallons) of oil fuel. In addition 37 steel tanks were built each capable of holding 5,000 tons of oil fuel.

The oil fuel reservoir (then with a multi arched roof) and fuel tanks in 1922.
The fuel tanks were demolished in 2004.
(Dunfermline Carnegie Library)

Following the Great War, the Treaty of Washington was drawn up and signed by the major powers in 1922. This restricted the size of the navies and as a result the Royal Navy scrapped many of it ships. One consequence of this was that there was not enough work to occupy all the Royal Dockyards. 'Short-time working' had already been introduced at Rosyth in 1921 and the following year the news came that some 3000 men (almost half the work force at Rosyth) were to be dismissed. In a letter to Dunfermline Town Council in May 1922, the Admiralty stated that the changed situation meant the indefinite postponement of the original plans for a great naval base and manning port with barracks, hospitals, training schools. However the unrivalled docks at Rosyth made it certain that Rosyth would be permanently used for docking capital ships of the fleet. Taken together with the oil storage facilities provided to make Rosyth a permanent fuelling base and the neighbouring magazine establishment at Crombie, the Admiralty felt that it was out of the question that Rosyth would be abandoned as a Naval Base. This assurance proved to be very short lived as in September 1925, it was announced that Rosyth and Pembroke Dockyards were to be placed on a care and maintenance basis. By the beginning of the following year the vast bulk of the work force had either been discharged or had returned to the Southern Dockyards. Some of the berths and docks were leased to ship breaking firms and this became the main activity in the Dockyard until the late 1930s.

Although some 1600 houses had been built for the new town of Rosyth during the period 1915-1918, many of the residents had been happy to continue living in the Tin Town houses. The original (western part) was demolished in 1924 as residents moved to the better houses in the eastern part when they became vacant and to the new houses in Rosyth. The houses in the eastern part were demolished a few years later.

Bibliography:

Inverkeithing High School, (1982), *The Story of Rosyth*, Stirling, Educational Resources Unit

Anderson, J., Rogers, M. & Law, A. (1999), *An Outline History of Rosyth Dockyard*, prepared as part of the Carnegie Dunfermline Trust's 20th Century Dunfermline Project (Local History Department of Dunfermline Carnegie Library)

The Garden City Philosophy

Felicity M Greenfields & Leonie Chalkley

To understand the social and aesthetic reasoning behind the formation of Rosyth Garden City and the Garden City Movement itself, you need to first look at the way Victorian cities were changing. During the Industrial Revolution, huge numbers of rural workers left the countryside and flooded into the cities, drawn by the prospect of better-paid jobs and greater prosperity in the growing textile, ship building and heavy engineering industries of the day. Whilst these workers hoped to find a better life, most found only poverty and hardship, crowded into inadequate housing in the form of the traditional Scottish tenement flats.

This is reflected in the 1861 Scottish census which shows that some 34% of Scotland's urban population were living in tenements, with as many as 1% of these having little or no access to natural daylight because windows had been 'bricked-up'[1]. This census also reveals that 64% of Scotland's entire population lived in one- or two-roomed houses. Indeed, migration from the country to the cities meant that, by 1871, Glasgow was the second largest city in Britain with a population of over 477,700 people. It was also the most densely inhabited urban location in Britain *(BBCi, 2004)*. Consequently, Glasgow, and other major industrial centres, were prime candidates for the outbreak of disease and social unrest.

So bad were the conditions that, today, the tenement blocks themselves are sufficient to evoke powerful images of 19th Century

---

[1] Bricking up windows was a way of reducing council rates – at that time these were calculated based on room sizes which was determined by the number of windows per building.

poverty, overcrowding and squalor. There is no doubt of the scale of these problems during the Victorian era.

The following extracts from the Dunfermline Journal show that Fife, too, had its problems with poverty and poor housing:

Dunfermline Journal, 30 May 1903

In these small towns [Lochgelly, Cowdenbeath, and other Fife mining villages] in spite of the plentiful supply of cheap land, housing conditions are little better than in the slums of large cities, and even the presence of fresh air does little to counteract the evils of bad sanitation and uncontrolled development.

The housing question seems to us to lie at the root of the great social problem. If the working-classes of the country were better housed, sections of them would not require to spend so many nights in the public-houses. The labourer needs a room where he can spend an hour in quietness as well as the professional man, and if the labourers of this country had their spare room there would very likely be less need than there is at present for "Gothenburgs" and the modern abominations which are dignified by the name of workmen's clubs.

The problems of social deprivation in the UK were so serious that in the late 1880s philanthropist Charles Booth mapped out the poverty and social conditions prevailing in London at the time. Booth attempted to identify the many problems of inner-city living resulting from social inequalities, overcrowding and poverty by plotting the levels of poverty and occupation types on to a map of London. Whilst his work and his map was focused on London, it can be taken as being an indication of the conditions common in most of the major industrialised centres at that time and served as the basis for his later calls for a universal Old Age Pension to help alleviate the appalling conditions his map detailed.

Section of Booth's 'Map Descriptive of London poverty, 1898-9'
(Courtesy of London School of Economics)

Victorian Britain saw some truly amazing engineering and architectural innovations. The industrial revolution brought with it demands from industry and from members of the emerging wealthy, middle classes for new things of the built environment. These new requirements generated a period of invention; a new breed of inventors, engineers, architects and builders emerged working with different materials and employing new techniques. Production methods were changed as weaving, for example, ceased to be a cottage industry and linen and cotton mills became mechanised. This gave rise to factory systems which made it more convenient for workers to be housed on site. This often resulted in men, women and children being committed into virtual industrial slavery.

However, even in this time of 'industrial slavery', this era of extremes of poverty and wealth, there were men and women of compassion who cared deeply about the conditions under which the 'common working people' were living.

Many social reformers, like Joseph Rowntree and George Cadbury, tried to address these problems. Social housing schemes were initially built in response to these changing social and industrial pressures. Whilst these reformers were business men, directly profiting from the industrial revolution, they were also philanthropists – men of conscience and religious persuasion. Both Cadbury and Rowntree were Quakers and, as such, they held a very real belief that the care of their workers had to be practical. Accordingly, they and others like them, set about building rural, factory villages ('humane accommodation') to house their workers and their families.

One such 'model' village was Bournville Garden Village. Constructed by Cadbury in 1878, it was built along environmentally-friendly as well as socially congenial lines. Its green spaces contrasted starkly against the industrialised cityscape of nearby Birmingham and reflected Cadbury's environmental and social concerns. Cadbury believed that the social problems of poverty, drinking and gambling would continue until and unless the issue of depressing and demoralising surroundings was addressed. At Bourneville Village, houses were 'grouped around cul-de-sacs or gardens ... [a] school, [a] hospital, reading rooms and wash houses were also built for the people in the village'. Even the house designs themselves were 'superior to working class homes at that time, having larger rooms and generous sized gardens' *(www.spartacus.schoolsnet.co.uk)*. These homes were to become the prototypes of those adopted by A H Mottram when he designed and built Rosyth's garden city *(Dymock, C., 1969)*. It was hoped that by adopting this style of housing, Rosyth would avoid the worst of the social problems.

The idea of planning out social problems was not new. Indeed, architects throughout the ages have strived to impose social order using the built environment by 'planning out the ugly so as to create or enhance natural surroundings by designing parks, waterways, roads, buildings' *(Encyclopedia Britannica, 2000)*.

It was against this backdrop of highly dense, insanitary Victorian cities and strongly influenced by the writings and work of John Ruskin and William Morris that Sir Ebenezer Howard (1850-1928) first began advocating his Utopian Garden Cities.

Howard, whilst never directly involved nor trained in the architectural profession, was deeply concerned about social issues. Like Cadbury, he believed passionately that "if each man could have his own house, a large garden to cultivate and healthy surroundings then ... there would be for them a better opportunity of a happy family life." Howard was concerned by the deteriorating social conditions in the towns as well as the depopulation of the countryside. In this respect, he saw garden cities as being the answer. Moreover, Howard's garden city concepts involved designs for organising people as well as commercial and domestic buildings. Many of his design concepts were centred on the layout of roads, houses and open spaces. *(ICOMOS-UK, 2002)*

In 1902, he published his book *Garden Cities of Tomorrow*. The stated aim of his garden cities was "to raise the standard of health and comfort of all true workers of whatever grade – the means by which these objects are to be achieved being a healthy, natural, and economic combination of town and country life" *(Cornell University Library, 2004)*.

View of Letchworth
(© First Garden City Heritage Museum, Letchworth)

Several attempts along partial garden city lines were made. However, it was Letchworth, to the north of London with its mixed-class cottage styled houses set in a variety of crescents and cul-de-sac patterns which was the first real attempt to realise Howard's garden city dream in its entirety *(Goodman, D. & Chant, G., 1999)*.

As well as being extremely practical in addressing issues of social welfare, Howard's garden cities were concerned with resource conservation and environmental management. In this respect, Howard saw garden cities as providing a solution to the seemingly piecemeal development and endless sprawl of many of the newly industrialised Victorian cities. He believed that for cities to be humane they had to be both functional as well as environmentally and aesthetically pleasing. *(www.spartacus.schoolsnet.co.uk)*.

Howard's design adopted a low-density approach. His garden cities were characterised by their unity of design and purpose, which catered for the cultural, aesthetic and practical needs of the inhabitants. Houses were to have their own front and rear gardens; there were to be shopping centres, libraries, reading rooms, hospitals, schools, churches, public buildings, playing fields, allotments, and open spaces. Large, well planned parks were to be located within easy walking distance from every house and the streets themselves were to be wide, open, tree-lined boulevards. Industrial estates were to be limited to the outskirts of the city where their fumes and noise would be less offensive to the city's inhabitants. Each garden city was to be surrounded by a wide green belt, to help lessen the effects of the industrial areas as well as ensuring that all residents had easy access to all the benefits of the neighbouring countryside.

Though Howard's garden city concept was not wholly unique in terms of planning for sustainable environments, it was nevertheless one of the first of its kind to attempt to tackle issues of urban density. In attempting to explain what he saw as the problems of urban life and how they might be addressed, Howard drew a diagram of three magnets, two of which he used to highlight the advantages and disadvantages of town and the advantages and disadvantages of country living respectively. *(Pile, S., Brook, C. & Mooney, G., 1999)*

The third magnet he used to show how the blending of the advantages of both town and of country with none of their disadvantages would result in a practical solution to the many urban problems and the creation of a form of sustainable city. For this to work, cities had to be planned at the outset, not simply left to grow in a piecemeal, chaotic manner at the whim of profit-orientated construction barons. *(Pile, S., Brook, C. & Mooney, G., 1999)*

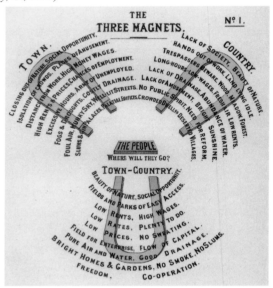

Ebenezer Howard's 'three magnets'
(© First Garden City Heritage Museum, Letchworth)

Howard's vision looked to manage the growth of cities. Each garden city was to be limited to some 32,000 people, a number he defined as the ideal population size for a city. Once this population level had been reached, his plan envisaged the formation of bio-regions – clusters of satellite cities surrounding the original city linked to each other by a network of railways *(Mumford, L., 1961)*. Such a concept was innovative in its ability to develop the garden village ideal into an adaptable, viable concept for creating humane city living.

Undoubtedly Howard had his critics. For the most part, these critics were from the social elite and were consequently able to readily commute to the country from the smog-bound and overcrowded city centres. They could therefore enjoy all the benefits of both city and country living. They saw no hypocrisy in their objection to the working classes experiencing this self-same blend of town and county living.

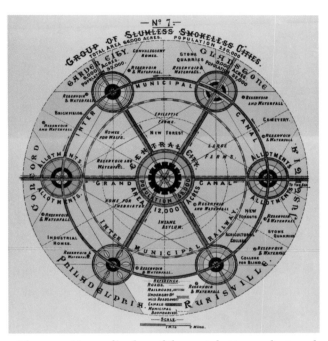

Ebenezer Howard's plan of the social city: a cluster of garden cities surrounding a central city.
(© First Garden City Heritage Museum, Letchworth)

Many of his critics also believed Howard to be anti-urban, though this was unfounded; Howard was perfectly aware that for cities to work in terms of vibrancy, they had to combine uniformity, variety, luxury, social amenities, tradition, sameness as well as difference. Nevertheless, Howard was equally aware that it was essential that some of the less welcome aspects of urban life such as pollution, poverty, squalor, crime and sickness had to be addressed. Cities, even today, need to combine levels of innovation, anonymity, freedom and dependency. Though many of the less desirable traits are evident in cities all over the world, it is essential to address such ever-present problems. Indeed, if such problems are left to fester they simply gnaw away at the vibrancy of city life, suspending social cohesion, generating unrest and generally having a detrimental effect upon the economic life of a city. *(Massey, D., Allen, J. & Pile, S., 1999)*

Howard's town planning legacy is immense. His influence can be traced, not only in the acknowledged garden cities such as Welwyn Garden City and Hampstead Garden Suburb but also in later post-War 'new towns'. For the latter, whilst the idea of 'building communities' remained, much of the architecture lost its 'green' feel and became instead concrete and steel monoliths, owing its architectural designs to a more modernist school.

One of the best known and most influential of this school was Charles-Edouard Jeanneret-Gris, (1887-1965), known as 'Le Corbusier'. As a central figure in modernist architecture circles, it is not surprising that Le Corbusier favoured hard-edged concrete, steel and glass buildings, constructed along geometric lines (Pile, S., Brook, C. & Mooney, G., 1999). From his perspective, tower blocks could be viewed as 'beautiful' because high density units fulfilled their function. They were, in his words, ' Machines for Living'.

In many respects, the adoption of 'best practice' meant that Le Corbusier style tower blocks were adopted by many local authorities for post-War reconstruction throughout the UK and abroad as the ideal way to house the maximum number of people using the least amount of space.

However, by the time of Le Corbusier's death in the mid-1960s, social problems that today, seem almost intrinsic in high-density living were becoming increasingly evident. This, coupled with a more environmentally aware public, has seen much of the modernist style rejected and a return to the 'greener', lower density, more 'people-orientated' theories of Ebenezer Howard.

If tenements had been built in Rosyth at the time of the Dockyard's construction, this undoubtedly would have solved the housing problem. Thankfully however, a far-sighted town Council resisted the desire to solve the accommodation shortage by building large multi-storey blocks of flats at Rosyth. Indeed, Dunfermline Town Council were ahead of their time in their belief that high-density living was likely to create more problems than it solved.

Considering the alternatives that might easily have resulted from the building of houses for the dockyard, it is a pity that there seems to be little appreciation or understanding of the importance and legacy of Howard's garden city concept as it relates to Rosyth.

Rosyth is not simply a collection of houses bounded by hedges and a public park with a few trees dotted here and there; it is more than that! It is the result of a well thought-out, planned garden city, a Utopian city, a social experiment.

Bibliography

BBCi (2004), *BBC - SOS Teacher - GSCSE Geography population and development,* [on-line] Available from: http://www.bbc.co.uk/schools/sosteacher/answers/answer35617.shtml [Accessed 09/03/2004]

Pile, S., Brook, C. & Mooney, G. (1999) *Understanding Cities: Unruly Cities*, Open University, Routledge, New York

Pile, S., Brook, C. & Mooney, G. (1999) *Understanding Cities: Unsettling Cities*, Open University, Routledge, New York

www.spartacus.schoolsnet.co.uk [Accessed March 2004]

Dymock, C. (1969) 'Rosyth Garden City Nears its Diamond Jubilee', *Dunfermline Press*, 12/09/1969

Mumford, L. (1961) *The City in History: Its origins, transformations and prospects*, MJF Books, New York

Encyclopedia Britannica Deluxe CD 2000 (1994-2000), *The Art of Architects*, Encyclopedia Britannica Inc., Published by britannica.co.uk

The Open University, (1999), *From Here To Modernity Architects - Le Corbusier*, [on-line] Available from: www.open2.net/modernity/4_1.htm [Accessed 15/03/2004]

Cornell University Library, *Garden Cities of Tomorrow - Ebenezer Howard*, [on-line] Available from: www.library.cornell.edu [Accessed 15/03/2004]

Goodman, D. & Chant, G. (1999), *European Cities & Technology: Industrial to post-industrial Cities,* Open University, Routledge, London

ICOMOS-UK (2002) *H@R!: Heritage at Risk 2002-2003*, [on-line] Available from: www.international.icomos.org/risk/2002/uk2002.htm, [Accessed 15/11/2003]

Massey, D., Allen, J. & Pile, S. (1999) *City Worlds: Understanding Cities,* Open University, Routledge, London

Rosyth Garden City

Felicity M Greenfields & Leonie Chalkley

To say that bureaucratic wheels turned slowly with regard to the planning and building of Rosyth town greatly understates the case. Whilst the Admiralty accepted and could even be said to have initially shown some enthusiasm for the Garden City plan, they were nevertheless unwilling to take on the financial implications of such a project. Consequently, a game of bureaucratic ping pong ensued between the Admiralty and the local authorities as to who was responsible for housing the expected 3,500 strong work force. *(The Story of Rosyth, 1982)*

As the principal landowner, the Admiralty was seen as being the most appropriate body to prepare a Town Planning Scheme for Rosyth. However, the Admiralty consistently stated that they had neither the resources nor the expertise to carry out the planning of the new town. They suggested that the Local Government Board for Scotland (LGB) should undertake the project. The LGB felt unable to do so because, as the arbitrators and final approving body, it was inappropriate for them to prepare a town planning scheme for their own approval. As far as the law was concerned, a town planning scheme should only be prepared by the landowner, in this case by the Admiralty. Moreover, the LGB did not feel able to undertake the planning process without extra resources and financial assistance which the Admiralty did not feel capable of supplying. *(SEP 15/2/7)*

The Edinburgh Branch of the Garden Cities & Town Planning Association, however, were keen to be involved in the project and approached the LGB in 1910. At the request of the Garden Cities Association, the Admiralty sent a plan of the area intended for the new town of Rosyth. This plan showed the land to the north of the newly constructed Admiralty Road as being the proposed area for housing. However, the Association responded by suggesting that this area was the "least suitable" and asking whether the Admiralty had considered the land to the south of the new road. The Admiralty advised that ultimately the southern portion of land was also intended for housing and shops *(SEP 15/2/7)*.

Letter from Lord Pentland to Right Hon. Reginald McKenna, MP

No doubt it is very much in the interests of the Government as a whole that we should see that the principles of town-planning which we have carried into law should if possible be successfully applied in the case of Rosyth. That town furnishes an early and a signal instance of the situation which the Act of 1909 was designed to meet, and the same Government which passed the Act is responsible for the creation of the new community. The steps taken at Rosyth will therefore be keenly watched by municipalities and by the public generally, and a successful application of town-planning principles will not only be of the highest value to the community directly concerned, but will afford an example of powerful influence over other Scottish cites where the old system, or the lack of system has produced deplorable results.

Of course it may be urged that the primary concern of the Admiralty is with ships and docks, and that town-planning is a matter rather of houses and streets. While that no doubt is true, it is also the case that, in this instance, the Admiralty, as leading landowner, seems to be the only authority capable of taking action in the initial stages; and, as you know, other good landowners and employers of labour have taken measures on town-planning lines to secure the healthy development of their land and the proper housing of their work people, even before the passing of the Act of 1909." *(SEP 15/2/4)*

At the request of the Local Government Board, the Edinburgh Garden Cities Association, began preparing a Town Plan for Rosyth for the land to the south of Admiralty Road. They went to considerable effort and expense in doing so, liaising with the LGB and the Admiralty throughout the process. At the latter's suggestion, they even visited Chatham and Devonport Dockyards in England to speak with both officials and workers so as to fully understand the requirements of worker housing and the rental levels which could be expected. In April 1910, they submitted their plans to the LGB, gaining general approval of the plan. The Association's costing of the project and of the expected returns in view of the necessarily low rents forced them to conclude that the project would become viable only if the Admiralty charged very low feu duties (ground rent) for the land. So, in November 1911, the Association asked the Admiralty for an indication of the feu duties that could be expected *(SEP 15/2/7)*.

Letter from LGB (Edinburgh) 22/4/12 to Sir James M. Dodds, Scottish Office

"... I do not think the First Lord can have realised the Admiralty's responsibility as to housing their own workmen. That responsibility cannot be shunted on to the Local Government Board. The crux of the matter, however, is what price are they prepared to take for the land? At the Board's official enquiry last week at Inverkeithing, it was stated in evidence by the convenor of the Town Planning Committee "that house rents in Inverkeithing had been increased by from 20 to 87 percent since work commenced at the Naval Base". Could not the Secretary for Scotland discuss this matter with the First Lord of the Admiralty? The question is certain to be raised in Parliament if something is not done to meet what everyone here realises will become a critical situation at no distant date.

The Admiralty's response was that Dunfermline Town Council had pledged to undertake their own Town Planning Scheme for Rosyth and that the Admiralty would await its completion. Then in January 1912, a notice in the public press appeared to the effect that the Admiralty's plans had changed and they now did not intend to release for housing the land to the south of Admiralty Road. The Garden Cities Association was understandably "aggrieved" considering the time and money they had expended on their Town Plan. They also did not consider that the Dunfermline Town Council plan would succeed, both because it was unlikely to be completed before the arrival of the workers at the new dockyard and because they felt that Dunfermline Town Council would be mainly concerned with the laying out of the ground with regard to the roads and the utilities such as water and drainage, rather than the construction of the actual houses themselves *(SEP 15/2/7)*.

By April 1912, matters had still not been resolved; neither the site nor the amount of feu duties had been agreed.

In 1913, the Admiralty appointed Sir Raymond Unwin (1863 - 1940) to prepare a detailed plan for Rosyth. Unwin was an important figure in UK housing and town planning. Together with Barry Parker, he had been responsible for the design of Letchworth, an embodiment of Sir Ebenezer Howard's garden city plans. He was also part of the pressure group responsible for bringing the first Housing and Town Planning Act (1909) into being, enabling local authorities to regulate the layout and density of suburban developments. In 1914, he became the Chief Town Planning Officer for the Local Government Board and, following the death of Howard in 1928, Unwin was to become President of the International Federation for Housing and Town Planning *(Letchworth Garden City, 2004)*.

Unwin brought much of his Quaker heritage to the task of designing Rosyth, fostering as he did a love for nature and a desire to see its benefits passed on to others. As an architect, he had a passion for pure clean lines and would incorporate and preserve nature into his plans whenever possible without losing sight of the economic necessities and the sociological issues *(Dymock, C., 1969)*. Unwin's plan for Rosyth consisted of low-density housing, with each house having its own front and back garden and the whole town encompassed by a wide green-belt area.

Despite Unwin's involvement, the planning for Rosyth still did not progress with any great speed. However, in 1914, with the threat of war looming in Europe, the Admiralty and Dunfermline Town Council finally came to an agreement.

Tenders to construct the new town were called for from private contractors but no suitable bids were forthcoming. As the case was now urgent, the Scottish National Housing Company (SNHC) was incorporated in October 1914 to carry out the building of Rosyth. The majority of the shares in the SNHC were held by Dunfermline Town Council and of the estimated £1 million cost for the project, 90% was loaned by the LGB with the Company responsible for the remainder.

However, further delays resulted from disputes between the various owners of the land and the LGB. Finally, with the Dockyard due to open in June 1915, the government stepped in, forcing through the Housing (Rosyth Dockyard) Act, effectively overriding local by-laws and building regulations in an effort to get things moving.

House style at Weoley Hill Estate. Bournville, Prototype of style for Rosyth.

The first houses to be built were designed by architects Greig and Fairburn, Edinburgh, over-seen by Mr. AM Mottram. Mottram was the ideal person to entrust with the work. Not only had he wide experience in community housing in South Wales and elsewhere but he had also been Unwin's assistant on the Hampstead Garden Suburb project from 1907-1912. With both Unwin and Mottram involved in the design and building of Rosyth, a garden city style town was pretty much assured.

Many of Mottram's innovative house plans borrowed heavily from homes which had been specifically created for Cadbury's Weoley Estate in Bournville village.

These cottages were vastly superior to the general quality of homes of their time and were in themselves very different from the row upon row of red-bricked terraced homes with which many of Rosyth's English workers would have been familiar.

View of Rosyth's Queensferry Road cottage-style housing, circa 1920

The first houses, built between the years 1915-1918, were of a traditional cottage design, with small windows and steeply pitched slate or tiled roofs. The frontages were well considered and the houses themselves had generous gardens. These gardens were edged with hedges of privet, holly and beech. As well as building houses in blocks of two, four and eight, Mottram's plan incorporated a variety of house designs so as to avoid the possibility of uniformity *(Inverkeithing High School, 1982).*

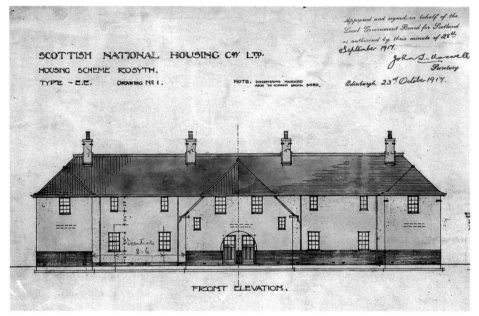

Detail of AM Mottram's architectural plans for Rosyth

Amongst the first houses built in Backmarch Road in Rosyth were some of type 'E' shown above. These houses were grouped around landscaped open spaces, parkland, and built along wide tree-lined streets *(Protecting Rosyth Garden City).*

Rosyth's Garden City Plan, as well as involving houses, also incorporated commercial, municipal, social and religious buildings. Whilst some of these structures were not built in the first phase of Rosyth's development, they were nevertheless an important part of a coherent whole. The Parkgate Institute, the Gothenburg (the 'Goth'), Rosyth's shops, the Palace Buildings and the Parish Church located on Queensferry Road were all part of Rosyth's planned development.

Rosyth Parish Church

The original plan was to build 3,000 houses over a six year period from 1915. Of these, only 1,872 were built between the years 1915 and 1919. The first 150 were built near Backmarch Road in 1916. Thereafter approximately 500 houses per year were built during the next three years. This was particularly remarkable considering war-time restrictions on both men and materials *(Begg, T., 1987)*.

It is fair to say that, despite the efforts to design houses suitable for the new dockyard workforce, the houses were not uniformly popular. Occupants complained about the lack of access to the rear gardens and of the awkwardly shaped rooms. The high rents were also criticised, despite the fact that rents at the 1915 level were still being charged in 1919. However, many of these criticisms were a form of 'architectural bigotry' as the houses, quite apart from being 'externally picturesque', were in fact 'found to have been extremely well built' *(Begg, T., 1987)*.

Unfortunately, Phase 3 of the Rosyth Town Plan never materialised as a result of the downturn at the Dockyard following the war. The houses that were built, however, quite apart from their superb workmanship and style, are a tangible reminder of early 20th century social housing development. They may well in themselves constitute a class of historic monument *(Dymock, C., 1969).*

Bibliography

Inverkeithing High School, (1982), *The Story of Rosyth*, Stirling, Educational Resources Unit

Goodman, D. & Chant, G. (1999) *European Cities & Technology: Industrial to post-industrial Cities,* Open University Course Book: AT308 Cities and Technology, Routledge: London

Begg, T, (1987), *50 Special years – A Study in Scottish Housing*, Canongate Publishing

Letter from Lord Pentland to Right Hon. Reginald McKenna, MP (1911), (Records held by Scottish Economic Planning Department, Ref. SEP 15/2/4)

Scottish Economic Planning Department, 15 2/4)

Letter from G. F. Henderson to Right Hon. Winston Spencer Churchill, MP (10/04/1912), (Records held by Scottish Economic Planning Department, Ref. SEP 15/2/7)

Letchworth Garden City (2004) *Sir Raymond Unwin (1863 - 1940)* [online], Available from: http://www.letchworthgardencity.net/heritage/index-6.htm [Accessed 25 March 2004]

Letter from LGB (Edinburgh) 22/4/12 to Sir James M Dodds, Scottish Office

Dymock, C. (1969) 'Rosyth Garden City Nears its Diamond Jubilee', *Dunfermline Press*, 12/09/1969

Dunfermline District Council, *Protecting Rosyth Garden City*, Dunfermline District Council Planning Department

The Second World War

Martin Rogers

In the years leading up to the Second World War, Rosyth Dockyard was still operating on a care and maintenance basis. It was the home for a number of First World War vintage destroyers held in reserve but the main activity in the Dockyard was the breaking up of ships by the commercial firm Metal Industries. This activity was to continue in a very limited way throughout the war and into the early sixties. Many famous ships of the Royal and Merchant Navies ended their days at Rosyth including HM Ships Ajax, Colossus, New Zealand, Agincourt and Princess Royal and the liners Mauretania and Leviathan. Also broken up in the docks at Rosyth were ships of the German Navy. After

The 49,000 ton liner Leviathan formerly owned by United States Lines arrives at Rosyth in 1938 to be broken up. She started life in a German shipyard as the Vaterland. (Douglas Cornhill)

they had been interned at Scapa Flow, many of the German ships were scuttled by their crews in June 1919. These ships were raised (mostly floating upside down) and the larger ones were towed to Rosyth to be scrapped.

In April 1937, Rosyth became the home for a new training establishment for artificers and boy seamen. It was given the name "HMS Caledonia" which had been used previously by a training ship in the Forth until 1906. As a temporary measure whilst permanent buildings were built, the former liner Majestic was converted into a floating barracks and classrooms and was moored on the west wall of the basin. In June 1937, trams were replaced by buses in the Dunfermline area and the line to Rosyth Dockyard was closed. It was announced in December 1938 that the Dockyard was to be opened up in a limited way and the following April saw the re-opening of the departments of the Dockyard.

As the threat of war with Germany increased, steps were taken to recruit and train people for Air Raid Precautions and Civil Defence duties. This began at the end of 1937 and continued throughout 1938 with lectures and demonstrations being given on various aspects of air raid precautions. Also in 1938, recruits were sought for anti-aircraft batteries which were being formed, one of which was sited to the west of Primrose Farm. Gas masks were issued to Rosyth residents in September and trenches were dug as makeshift shelters. Amidst the preparations for war, life went on and in the summer of 1938 the paddling pool was opened in the Public Park. This was to become a popular spot for youngsters to play in the summer months. In 1939 work started on building a police station at the Crossroads although with wartime restrictions, it was not opened until May 1943.

On the housing front, Dunfermline Town Council drew up plans for a new estate of 182 houses near Rosyth Halt (Wemyss Street and Nelson Street). Work started at the beginning of 1939 and the first houses were occupied in July of that year. Although not originally intended for this purpose, many of the houses when completed were occupied by non-

Rosyth Remembered

"We used to go down and watch them build the paddling pool. They used pneumatic spades, like a pneumatic drill but with a spade instead of a spike on the end. They built a little bridge with railway lines and sleepers across the burn to the land between the burn and the backs of the houses in Parkside Street and they dumped the clay all the way along there. When they'd finished filling up that bit they dumped it on the land between Parkgate and the Palace. The clay was lovely - it was like Plasticine. We used to roll it into balls and have battles. Eventually the paddling pool was finished and it was filled by water from the burn which ran beside Burnside Place. They built a sluice, a dam, and put wooden boards into a slot which dammed the burn and allowed the water to come up through a pipe under Park Road and into the paddling pool." *Frank Pope*

Houses in Wemyss Street under construction in April 1939
(Dunfermline Journal)

Admiralty workers who had been given notice to quit their houses in the Garden City part of Rosyth. This was to make way for incoming Admiralty workers from the southern Dockyards. Even with these extra houses, housing for Admiralty workers was still in very short supply and many workers had to be found lodgings in Edinburgh.

In June 1939, the Home Fleet and a squadron of French warships visited Rosyth. Some of the ships were open to visitors and a newspaper report states that some 10,000 people visited the Dockyard to see the ships at close quarters. The clock tower on Pease Hill was erected that month. Standing 22 feet high, it replaced a clock tower which had formerly surmounted the Royal Navy Canteen in Admiralty Road. The Home Fleet again visited Rosyth in August during its autumn cruise. At the same time, train loads of reservists arrived to take over 10 ships which had been in reserve at Rosyth, mostly V and W Class destroyers. They were heading for Weymouth Bay where the King was due to carry out an inspection of reservists and ships of the Home Fleet.

Children from Park Road School being evacuated in September 1939
(Dunfermline Journal)

Plans had been prepared for the evacuation of children from Rosyth because of its proximity to the Dockyard. When war was declared on

3 September 1939 these plans were put into operation with many of the Rosyth children being evacuated to Strathmiglo, Auchtermuchty, Leslie, Markinch and Falkland. The boy seamen being trained at HMS Caledonia were transferred to the Isle of Man but the artificers moved ashore to King's Road School which was requisitioned for this purpose. HMS Caledonia was considered too much of a hazard to remain in the Dockyard because of her size and she was towed out into the Forth where she had water pumped into her bilges so that she sat on the river bottom. One report suggests that she was to be used as a troop ship but this was not to be as she caught fire a short time later.

Rosyth Remembered

"The blackout used to be a bit of fun especially if you bumped into somebody. It was "oops, sorry, you all right? I'm all right, you all right? Yes, goodbye." Headlights on the cars were absolutely useless. You were allowed to carry a torch but it had to have either two or three thickness of tissue paper over the lens, so it didn't guide you anywhere. All it did was show that there was somebody there with a torch which did help a bit. You could also get luminous badges, which you held up to the light before you went out, pinned them on your coat and they glowed mauve for a period before they faded."
Frank Pope

Warden posts for Air Raid Precautions (ARP) were set up in Will's Garage in Park Road, Middlebank Street, Castlandhill and King's Crescent. Properly constructed air raid shelters were provided. Individual houses had corrugated iron Anderson shelters or steel-topped box structures (Morrison shelters). Communal ones were provided throughout Rosyth and at public buildings. A decontamination depot was established at the Backmarch Steading and a first aid post in one of the Masonic Halls. A Sub Station of the National Fire Service (more commonly known as the Auxiliary Fire Service) was located in Rosyth (also based at Will's garage) and a force of 250 Special Constables was established in Dunfermline Burgh with four of the fifteen sections based in Rosyth. They undertook patrol work, one particular duty being the enforcement of blackout regulations.

There was something of an anti-climax after the declaration of war with no sign of enemy activity. This changed on 16 October when German bombers attacked Royal Naval ships in the Firth of Forth (not the Forth Bridge as is often stated). This was the first raid anywhere in mainland Britain. The raid was repulsed with two of the German planes being shot down but not before inflicting some casualties on the ships in the Forth. The worst hit was the destroyer HMS Mohawk which was damaged by machine gun fire and splinters from a bomb which narrowly missed the ship. Sixteen of her crew were killed, including her Captain and some of these were buried with military honours in Douglas Bank cemetery.

Sailors at graves of their comrades at Douglas Bank Cemetery in October 1939
(Dunfermline Journal)

This early attack on the Forth was not a sign of things to come. Despite its importance as a Naval Base, Rosyth was to escape relatively lightly so far as air raids were concerned. There were over 100 air raid warnings during the war but in most cases there was no bombing or anti-aircraft fire. There is only one recorded incident of bombing in Rosyth (in April 1941) and three in Dunfermline (the earliest in August 1940 and the latest in April 1942).

In 1939, the Scottish National Housing Company began work on building 134 houses in King's Road. At that time the road did not exist and the dual carriageway and service roads were built at the same time as the houses at a cost of just under £19,000. By the end of 1940, about 88 houses were occupied and the remainder were almost complete although the roadworks were not.

Rosyth Remembered

"I went to King's Road School and when the war started the school closed and it was taken over by the Navy. We hung about the streets for two or three months or maybe even longer. Before the Navy actually went in there all the books etc. had to be removed from the school. I don't know how we were notified - it must have just been by word of mouth - but anybody with a bike was told to report to King's Road School. So we did, and our saddlebags and school bags were all filled with books and we cycled to Limekilns School and deposited them there." *Frank Pope*

Many of the school children who had been evacuated, returned to Rosyth within a few months. Schooling was difficult as most of the schools had been commandeered for naval and military purposes. Park Road School was used by the RAF to house the men operating the balloon barrages and King's Road School housed the artificer apprentices of HMS Caledonia. From the beginning of 1940, St. John's

RC School was used by Protestant and Roman Catholic children. A shift system operated with the children attending for only part of the morning or afternoon. Some of the King's Road pupils and teachers went to Inverkeithing School and then to Queen Anne School. Two nurseries were opened by the Town Council in August 1942 - at Broomhead Park in Dunfermline and in Rosyth. The Rosyth one was a temporary wooden building erected in the Public Park at Harley Street.

Pitreavie Castle had been bought by the Air Ministry in 1938 and became the headquarters of 18 Group Coastal Command. An underground bunker was completed in 1941, housing the Maritime Headquarters with Royal Air Force and Royal Navy staff working in close co-operation. The hunt for the Bismarck and raids against shipping in occupied Norway were planned here and the Battle of the Atlantic was largely mounted from here.

Constructing the underground bunker at Pitreavie Castle in 1941
(Inverkeithing Local History Society)

Members of the Rosyth Home Guard in December 1944 after the stand down parade.
(Dunfermline Journal)

Rationing was introduced in January 1940 - initially restricted to sugar, butter, bacon and ham. Over the next two years this was extended to include cooking fat, meat, tea, cheese, jam, eggs, sweets and clothing. To try to compensate for food shortages a "Dig for Victory" campaign encouraged households to cultivate allotments and keep poultry.

The Local Defence Volunteers were formed in May 1940 when there were threats of invasion. They later changed their name to the Home Guard and the 7th Fife Battalion of the Home Guard was established to cover West Fife with its headquarters in Dunfermline. There were four Companies in the Battalion with A Company centred on Dunfermline and including the town of Rosyth. Initially there was a separate E Company for the Dockyard but this was absorbed into a special Dockyard Battalion - the 9th Fife Battalion. The reason for this change was that the Home Guard were issued with a .300 rifle whereas Naval personnel were armed with a .303 rifle. It was felt that the Dockyard Home Guard should be armed and munitioned to Admiralty standards.

The Home Guard were demobilised in December 1944 and a stand down parade was held to mark the occasion.

Most public buildings in Rosyth were used for war time activities. The Church of Scotland's hall was used as a canteen and rest room for the forces. A room in the Methodist Church in Parkgate was used for a Women's Voluntary Service sewing and knitting group. The Methodist and Baptist Churches together with the Co-op Hall at the Crossroads were designated as rest centres in the event of families being made homeless by bombing raids. About thirty people were recruited to run each of the centres should the need arise. The Churches and other buildings were also used as additional school classrooms.

Casualties being taken into Parkgate Institute during an exercise in November 1939
(Dunfermline Journal)

The barrage balloons protecting Rosyth Dockyard were particularly susceptible to damage and in June 1940 during a severe thunderstorm, eight balloons were struck by lightning and destroyed. In February of the following year high winds dislodged eighteen balloons from their moorings and all were destroyed.

VIPs outside Rosyth Parish Church during the
Wings for Victory Parade in April 1943
(Dunfermline Journal)

Salvage collection was a major preoccupation and would put modern efforts at re-cycling very much in the shade. A press report in August 1941 records that during July, 83 tons of material had been salvaged and sold in the Dunfermline area realising almost £360. Paper formed the bulk of this but there were also bones, bottles, glass, pig food, rags, manure and scrap metal. Organisations such as the Boy Scouts and Boys' Brigade were very much involved in this kind of activity.

Fund raising was an ongoing business during war time. Money was raised for causes such as the Red Cross, Comforts for HM Forces, Prisoners of War Fund, Nursing Fund and the Ambulance Fund. In addition there were special campaigns to raise money or encourage investment in Saving Certificates and Defence Bonds. There were four major campaigns - a War Weapons Week in June 1941, a Warship Week in April 1942, a Wings for Victory Week in April 1943 and a Salute the Soldier Week in April 1944. Together with a Tanks for Attack effort in October 1942, a total of over £2,300,000 was raised in Dunfermline Burgh. In Rosyth during the Wings for Victory Week the fund raising activities held included a grand pageant, four grand dances, four concerts, a military whist drive, a keep fit display and a film display. The proceeds from these events were invested on behalf of the Dunfermline and West Fife Hospital.

Beatrice Lilley and Evelyn Lay with sailors after the opening of the Royal Navy and Royal Marine Canteen in the Dockyard in March 1941.
(Photograph courtesy of the Imperial War Museum, London A3128)

A number of buildings were opened in Dunfermline and Rosyth to provide opportunities for servicemen to relax and enjoy their off duty time. There was a canteen in the Dockyard itself and in Rosyth there were the YMCA's premises at the corner of Castle Road and Ferrytoll Road, the Rest Centre in Rosyth Parish Church and the British Sailors'

Society's hostel in Castle Road (now the Forth Club) which opened in 1941. Unfortunately one of the leisure time activities had unwanted consequences prompting occasional public health warnings in the local press about the dangers of venereal disease. Regular Garrison Theatre concerts were held in the Co-op Hall in Admiralty Road as well as many other concerts and dances, some being held for fund raising purposes. Visits to the Dockyard by ENSA were very much appreciated and among the well known artistes who appeared at Rosyth were Evelyn Laye, Beatrice Lillie and Gracie Fields.

An early view of Dollytown houses in October 1942
(Rosyth and Inverkeithing Journal)

The pressing need for additional housing for Dockyard workers led the Admiralty to build houses in the fields to the south of Admiralty Road and between Castlandhill Road and Castle Road. These were built in 1942 and were single storey flat roofed houses which became popularly known as Dollytown. There is a remarkable parallel between Dollytown and the Tin Town of the First World War. Both developments

The Prime Minister, Winston Churchill, acknowledges the cheers of Dockyard workers on a visit to the Dockyard in October 1940.
(Photograph courtesy of the Imperial War Museum, London A1483)

King George VI carrying out an inspection at Rosyth in March 1941.
This was probably on board HMS Hood, one of two ships he visited.
(Photograph courtesy of the Imperial War Museum, London A3367)

were supposed to be temporary but lasted for many years (in the case of Dollytown, over 30 years) and, like the Tin Town residents, many Dollytown residents developed great affection for their homes.

During and shortly after the war, there were many visits to the Dockyard by national and international figures. These included General Sikorski (Polish Premier and Commander in Chief) in November 1939, Winston Churchill (Prime Minister) and Mrs. Churchill in October 1940, King George VI in April 1940, King George VI and Queen Elizabeth in March 1941 and in March and September 1945 and Field Marshal Sir Bernard Montgomery in November 1945. Prince Olav of Norway left from Rosyth to return to Norway in May 1945 and was followed by his father, King Haakon, and other members of the Royal Family in June.

The aircraft carrier, HMS Indomitable in the basin in May 1944.
She is manoeuvring to enter No 2 dock.
(Photograph courtesy of the Imperial War Museum, London A23377)

The Dockyard played a crucial role in repairing and refitting ships of the Royal Navy and of allied countries. The work force peaked at

8,000 men and 2,000 women working a 63 hour week with day and night shifts. An early casualty in need of the Dockyard's services was HMS Belfast which was temporarily repaired after striking a mine in the Forth. Rosyth was the main assembly port for the Norwegian Expedition in April 1940 (the attempt to prevent the invasion of Norway by Germany). Over 1,200 vessels were ammunitioned and stored.

An early shift of workers leaving the Dockyard in August 1944.
(Photograph courtesy of the Imperial War Museum, London A25208)

The pride of the Royal Navy, HMS Hood, was at Rosyth in March 1941 shortly before meeting her fateful end in the clash with the German ship Bismarck. All five battleships of the King George V Class and some of the new fleet aircraft carriers came to Rosyth from the shipbuilders for fitting out before going on active service. It is estimated that over 3,000 ships (including at least one Russian submarine) were refitted at Rosyth. As well as refitting and repairing naval ships, the Dockyard undertook a large amount of industrial production, installing machinery at shore establishments, reconditioning power units and salvaging many thousands of expensive machinery items.

After the D-Day landings in June 1944, increasing attention was being given to the post-war situation. The shop stewards in the Dockyard were anxious to forestall any attempt to close the Dockyard as had happened after the First World War. They produced a booklet which was sent to MPs, local authorities and representative bodies arguing for the publication of plans to deal with the future of the Dockyard. In September, a representative meeting of local authorities, trades unions and Members of Parliament was held in Dunfermline and in November a deputation met the First Sea Lord to press Rosyth's case for a role in the post-war situation.

In May 1945, hostilities with Germany ceased and Victory in Europe (VE) Day was celebrated on Tuesday 9 May spilling over to the Wednesday. In Rosyth most of the shops were closed and shops and houses were decorated with bunting. In the evening there was dancing and singing in the streets and many bonfires were lit. Effigies of Hitler were everywhere, some being placed on top of bonfires. A large party of young folk paraded through the main thoroughfares singing popular songs, dances were held in public halls and services of thanksgiving were held in the local Churches morning and evening. Similar celebrations were held on 15 August (VJ Day) when the war against Japan came to an end. The question then was 'what did the future hold for Rosyth town and Dockyard?'

Bibliography

"Metal Industries: Shipbreaking at Rosyth and Charlestown" (1992), Ian Buxton, The World Ship Society.

"Dunfermline During the War" - a series of articles in the Dunfermline Press between May 1945 and January 1946

Rosyth Remembered

Irene's Story

My brother Harry, aged six years, and me Irene, aged seven years, were evacuated to Leslie at the start of the Second World War as were many other children from Rosyth. I don't think that we really knew what was going on, not like children of today.

We had a trial march up to Rosyth Halt with our gas masks in a case round our shoulders and name tags attached to us; I think they were like tie on luggage labels.

Several days later the evacuation took place and we landed in a hall in Leslie. I remember the women in the WVS uniforms rushing around, we were in a daze. Then this very nice woman (Mrs. Anderson) came up and said she would take me and another girl, Harry started crying so she relented and took both of us.

Mrs. Anderson was the wife of the local doctor so we landed in Bank Place House, Leslie, a large stone built house with a garden and many trees. You could smell the foliage as you walked up the path. We were given a large room upstairs and during our stay we were looked after by the two maids in the house and spent a fair amount of time in the kitchen. All the windows had blackout shutters, which were closed when darkness began to fall.

Harry was very upset with the shutters in the bedroom one night and pleaded with me to take them down. Mrs. Anderson was upstairs in a fury. The Air Raid Warden was at the door complaining about the light showing. We stayed for about six months as everyone thought the war would soon be over. Our mother visited every Sunday; someone gave her a lift in their car.

During our stay we were off school quite a lot as Harry had whooping cough and I had impetigo, a very unpleasant skin infection - you had to have the scabs picked off and be plastered with Gentian Violet.

One of the maids took us to a farmhouse for tea one Sunday afternoon. The farmhouse belonged to a relative of hers.

We had one Christmas in Leslie and Dr. Anderson and his partner, Dr. Inglis, visited us and gave us presents. I think the two doctors surgeries were part of the house which is now a residential home. I look at it every time I pass through Leslie.

The Doctor's house was sumptuous compared with ours, carpets on the floors and heavy curtains. At home it was linoleum and a fireside rug but we were glad to be back. Harry ate a whole tin of biscuits on the day be returned (probably a week's supply) and he wasn't told off.

I came back with a very large Teddy which one of the doctors had won at a fun fair.

In the late 1930s and early 1940s we attended Park Road Primary School. We walked to school - no buses and very few cars. I think only two families in Woodside Avenue possessed a car.

Two boys from a large family near us walked to school in bare feet, no socks or shoes. I can still see them picking their way gingerly along Woodside Avenue and Middlebank Street. The boys were also very poorly clad. I remember the teacher asking some of the children from well-off families to find out if their parents had any spare clothes for the needy children in the class (no help from Social Security in that day and age).

We all had a small bottle of milk at playtime. There was a cardboard top on the milk with a small perforated area for your straw.

When the weather was cold we ran home to a big coal fire (lovely), no central heating for many years to come. At night our mother carried a shovel of hot coals upstairs to the bedroom fire so the room would be warm when we went to bed.

We did not go away on holiday but we went to Port Laing and Aberdour quite a lot. You could light a fire for your kettle at Port Laing (using driftwood) but this was not allowed at Aberdour so we took thermos flasks. We also had trips on the Ferry to South Queensferry, playing in the rock pools and walked towards Cramond. Occasionally our mother would take us to visit a small shop which sold Crest China and we would take ages deciding which pieces to buy.

We made our own entertainment. We had (with a few friends) concerts in the back garden. We hung two old blankets on a line as curtains for the stage. We invited an audience (a very small one) and I think the charge was a jam jar, we could get a halfpenny for it at the shops.

Woodside Avenue at its junction with Woodside Street c. 1920

We also played Bebs (Hopscotch) and skipping. When we were nine or ten years old we would go for walks, jump the burns and climb trees. We called ourselves the Woodside Avenue Gang, about seven or eight of us. We were scared stiff of the Wemyss Street Gang and would run for our lives when we saw them coming. We also tried baking potatoes in the woods in a banked area away from the trees, the skins were burnt but the potatoes were not well cooked.

We attended Church and Sunday school and went for walks on a Sunday afternoon along Primrose Lane (out in the country, no houses at that time). I remember the oak trees and picking the acorns.

My brother's Sunday school teacher told ghost stories to the children. My brother would gather a small group of us under the lamp post (small gas lamps) he would repeat the ghost stories to us then we would all run home. (The Sunday school teacher is now a resident in Leys Park Nursing Home and remembers the ghost stories.) We would go guising in fairly elaborate home made costumes and also went carol singing at Christmas. We had home-made sledges and walked up to Pitreavie golf course to sledge.

We were also very fond of reading and made regular visits to the library. There was no television and we didn't have a wireless until we were around about ten years old.

A friend's father had a magic lantern, pictures projected on a screen, and we were asked along to see it. I think the only film he had was about Malta, the George Cross Island.

Our grandfather had an allotment so we had a plentiful supply of vegetables and mother was a very good cook. We had lovely home-made soup with brose and the stovies were marvellous. Home-made toffee before the war but the sugar rationing put a stop to it.

On Saturday afternoons we would go to the Matinee at the Picture House. Roy Rogers, East Side Kids and Charlie Chaplin.

We hung socks up at the fireplace for Santa at Christmas. Ludo, Snakes and Ladders, painting or crayons and reading books, sweets and cut out dolls for me and an orange, we were always very excited and pleased with what we received.

Post-War Rosyth

Pat Callaghan

To fully appreciate the development of any phase of Rosyth's growth as Scotland's only Garden City we must direct ourselves to the following extract from the first Annual General Meeting of the Edinburgh Branch of The Garden City and Town Planning Association in May 1910 where Professor Lodge referred to:

"...the exciting problem of Rosyth. Here [we have] on land owned or partly owned by the State the prospect of building up a very considerable dockyard town".

The 1950s played its part in the building up of "this very considerable dockyard town".

It must also be remembered that this statement was the precursor to the State getting involved in subsidising public housing in the UK, sowing the seeds of what we now know as the Fife Special Housing Association. From little acorns ...?

In an early 1950s Dunfermline Press article there was reference to the 'supposed' run down of the Royal Dockyard at that time. The Provost of the day (Provost J. Stewart Gellatly) was giving the editor a real political 'doing' for 'continually crying "wolf" with regard to the future of the dockyard'. Provost Gellatly stated that Rosyth Dockyard was in no danger, but, if such a situation did arise, the first people on the job would be their Member of Parliament, the Town Council, and the Dockyard Retention Campaign Committee. "We know that Rosyth is safe for quite a good few years to come and to start an agitation would only be like cutting off our own noses to spite our own faces". Halcyon days! (*Dunfermline Press, 1950*)

It would seem that there was amongst us that breed who had both the potential and propensity to be spies! I refer, of course, to an incident in 1950 whereby a welder (Mr. John Copeland) was suspended from work in a "McCarthy" like swoop by our spy masters because he was a communist! (Burgess and MacLean were not communists nor welders!) Mr. Copeland was suspended for fourteen days with pay because of his associations with the Communist Party and because he had been a Communist Party candidate in the 1949 County Council elections. In a letter to the editor of the Dunfermline Press, Mr. Copeland protested against his "unjust" suspension saying that "my work as a welder is straightforward, and in no sense is it security work ... there is nothing against me as a workman" (*Dunfermline Press, 1950*). Paid for his skills - punished for his ideals! No change there, then!

Building work on new Cash Office in the Dockyard was almost complete when this
photo was taken in June 1957
(Morris Allan Collection at Dunfermline Carnegie Library)

The 1950s saw a significant amount of innovation and development in the dockyard with the building of the Apprentices Hostel (opened

Aug. 1956), Cash Office (Nov. 1957), the opening of the Apprentices Training Centre (Sep. 1957) and the Electrical Engineering workshop (Dec. 1958), building of married quarters for Naval personnel in Hilton Road (1955) and – in the interests of balance with all this development, no doubt – we also saw the YMCA Naval Institute burned down.

Following on from the war it was soon to become apparent that stealth operations would come to the fore in the subsequent "cold war" in the shape of submarines, rather than by air. Rosyth already had war experience of refitting submarines and it soon became obvious that it had a strategic role in the defence of the UK. The result was investment.

Earl Mountbatten of Burma, the First Sea Lord, on a visit to Rosyth in September 1957

In 1955 Rosyth Dockyard stopped generating its own electric supply and it was piped in from the national grid. Around this time it was recognised that it would be a substantial player in refits of our submarine fleet. The first submarine, HMS Sleuth, duly arrived in March 1955. This, of course, set up a long association between the MOD and Fife in terms of significant economic investment in the Region and its people. Countless thousands of jobs, futures, houses and dreams were secured in the area because of this liaison. The Dockyard found itself the owner of a revitalised national celebrity status owing to its strategic role in the defence of the UK and this in turn led to a series of high profile visits to the base. A particular and tragic royal favourite of mine who visited the base in August of 1955 was Earl Mountbatten of Burma and his wife, in his capacity of First Sea Lord. What a pity his life was brought to such a tragic conclusion and in such a devastating fashion.

Rosyth has always had strong links to our Royal family with many visits and stop-offs taking place here. In June 1955, for example, Queen Elizabeth and the Duke of Edinburgh departed from Rosyth on board the Royal Yacht Britannia on a state visit of Norway.

A lovely story, hopefully apocryphal (but I suspect not!) is one concerning the Royal Yacht Britannia which was undergoing minor repairs in June 1958 at the Base. Apparently our workmen, on board to do repairs, were issued with lovely brown overalls and white tennis plimsolls and given brand new tools inclusive of "hammers with rubber heads" to keep down noise levels!

On a lighter and perhaps more typical note we need to revert to the MOD "shakers and movers" - yes, the Planners!

A first-class example of forward planning occurred in early 1956 when the aircraft carrier, HMS Glory, was fully refitted at Rosyth only to be laid up in 1957 and scrapped at Inverkeithing in 1961. Well, at least we got the work! Another demolition took place in 1958 at the main gate of the Yard; Taffy's Shop, the old wooden newspaper/general store was demolished, being replaced by a brick built one. Progress.

The Dockyard staffing numbers and workload seemed to go up and down on an almost annual basis. Between 1951 and 1952 a figure of 8,000 employees, dropped to 5,600, despite a good workload and assurances from the Flag Officer that the capacity of the Yard was limited only by the numbers of people employed there. It is also interesting to note that, in 1953, 500 civilian workers 'invaded' Rosyth from Tyneside to fit out the interior of HMS Albion. Our landladies, apparently, were happy enough at the prospect of full houses but I suspect our wee communist in the welding shop wasn't!

During this period there was also a dearth of available housing for skilled workers.

Letter to The Editor, Dunfermline Press
18 March 1950
Dockyard Housing Problem

Perhaps, through your columns, you might bring to notice the hundreds of people waiting for a dockyard house.

I am a dockyard employee and have waited three years for a house. At present there are miners, builders, teachers and many more from overseas who are not employed by the Admiralty. Is it not a fact that all tenants sign a form to the effect that, on leaving the yard, they will give up their houses?

Perhaps our Provost will back up dockyard housing officials by finding other houses for those who are not entitled to dockyard houses. *Fed-up with Rooms*

Throughout the UK there was national need for new housing, partly to replace houses damaged in bombing raids but also to cater for an expanding population. Traditional building materials were in short supply and so new types of houses were designed. In the late 1940s and early 1950s, a number of new housing schemes started in Rosyth, many of them using these new designs. In the Burnside area, work began in 1948 on 120 houses with 70 of them being of the Whitson Fairhurst type (which used a concrete frame) and 50 of the BISF type (which had a frame of structural steel). Also in that year, work began on building 50 temporary bungalows (or prefabs) in Camdean made of aluminium and manufactured by ex-aircraft factories. In 1949, 60 Blackburn flatted-type houses were built in Camdean with walls constructed of brick but with the roof and some of the internal partitions made from a light alloy and in the early 1950s Millar Space saving houses were erected in the Park Road (West) area.

Rosyth was a hive of activity at this time; it was a time of retail development for the Garden City with many local businesses expanding and some new ones emerging, especially along the frontage opposite the "Palace" on Queensferry Road at the "Queens Buildings". Six new tennis courts were opened in Rosyth Public Park (June 1949) and a new Crown Post Office opened at the Crossroads in March 1952 In 1956 a new clubhouse for the Rosyth Bowling Club and a new hall for the Church of Scotland were opened.

Mrs. McRobb of Middlebank Street braves the floods
to buy her milk from the Co-op cart
(Lena Morris)

The Dockyard and its environs would never have survived without the people of Rosyth, the mainspring of its continuing success as a maritime port. Neither, of course, would the town itself have prospered without these good people and it is important to take a view of them as well.

The following snapshots of Rosyth and its people come mainly from the archives of the Dunfermline Press from 1950 – 1959 and make for some very interesting reading.

In September 1950, would you believe, we had problems with flooding in Rosyth? Children at Park Road Primary were in danger of being marooned and were therefore removed from the school. I wonder how many of today's Rosyth adults were those children? It was reported that the water was at some points more than a foot deep but that in the boiler room it was between 6' and 7' in depth. By 10.30 am. the only access was via a thin strip of dry land and so the pupils and teachers were forced to evacuate the school. Exciting memories!

In the same year, we had farmers and educationalists arguing over whether or not Rosyth should have a new primary school west of King's Road. This was manifested the next year when plans were passed in August 1951 for a new school at a cost of £114,000. The new school was opened on 14 September 1953 by Dr. DM McIntosh, Director of Education for Fife. During the opening ceremony Rev. W. Flint, Convenor of Fife Education Committee commented that "[Parents] were now setting their children in surroundings where they would learn the lessons of life, where they would learn how to live in a highly complex community, and, as a by-product of modern education, to play their part in a highly industrial age. The architect of Camdean School had achieved in wonderful measure the incarnation of those ideals of education." But Rev. Flint had obviously not spent any great time in the school. The 1950s architects, although comparatively much cheaper than today, did Camdean Primary no favours at all by their insistence on wall to wall glass. The result: really hot uncomfortable sunny days and freezing dull days!

On 2 June 1953 Rosyth, like the rest of Great Britain, (and indeed the Commonwealth), celebrated the Coronation of Queen Elizabeth II. Despite the continuation of post-War rationing of some food items, street parties were held throughout the Garden City. Streets such as Burnside Crescent and Norval Place were gaily decorated with buntings and flags and games and races were the 'norm'. Prizes of Coronation mugs filled with sweets, Coronation commemorative crown pieces and boxes of chocolates were presented to many lucky Rosyth children and fifteen old-age pensioners from the Burnside Crescent area even received the precious gift of a ¼ pound of tea! Parades and processions through the streets of Rosyth were a big feature of the day, in many cases led by local brass and pipe bands. Many street parties rounded off their celebrations with dancing and singing, accompanied by local artistes, by piano or even by phonograph. Food in the form of ices, jellies and teas were served throughout the day. No doubt amounts of certain stronger beverages were also consumed, although this was not reported in the local press - I wonder why!

Coronation Day Celebrations in Findlay Street, Rosyth
(Courtesy of Mr. W Hutchinson)

In the course of my research for this chapter, I came across a quaintly eerie report concerning the HMS Glory. During her refit in 1956, a painter's labourer, Mr. Harry Myerthall, would seem to have come face to face with an apparition in one of the ship's cabins. Mr. Myerthall had just stepped into the cabin to plug in a lamp when he saw a man approximately 5' 9" tall dressed in tropical flying kit - blue shorts and a leather flying jacket with a flying helmet on the back of his head. Thinking that the man was a member of the ship's staff, Mr. Myerthall greeted him but gained no response. Mr. Myerthall stepped back into the passageway but, realising that it was odd that a member of the ship's staff should be in the cabin, turned back to ask who he was. But the cabin was empty! A thorough search of the cabin did not locate him; he had disappeared! Following the incident, many speculated that it was the spirit of an officer killed whilst attempting to land on board the "Glory" during her tour of duty in the Korean conflict. Senior naval personnel on board at the time played down the sighting, denying that the ghost-figure had been seen twice previously. However, no explanation for the mysterious presence was ever forthcoming (*Dunfermline Press, 1956*).

Whilst on the subject of dark forces, a paradoxical report 'came to light' in an article showing new lamp standards being erected in Rosyth (at a massive cost of £35 each!) owing to it having 'the worst lit streets' in the Burgh; according to Bailie Elder there were only five lights in King's Road! *(Dunfermline Press, 1950)*. Rosyth received over 20 lamp standards.

I would assume that some of these lamps found their way to the front of the local dance hall – the old Co-op halls, otherwise known as 'The Snakepit'. Having spoken to many teenagers of that era I have to conclude that the regular influx of "tiffies" was not always a welcome sight in the area, either for dancing or romancing! 'The Snakepit' was located south of Admiralty Road above shops owned by the Co-Op and could boast regular full houses. It is interesting to note that this predominantly weekend venue (with a £0 2s 6d entry fee) was also unlicensed!

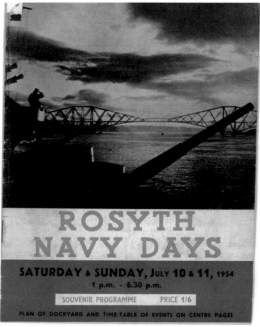

Navy Days Souvenir Program, 1954

In concluding this section, mention has to be made of the ubiquitous 'Navy Days' at the Dockyard. Every year we all waited for this highlight to come around, to allow access to our Royal Dockyard and 'get on the boats'. Some of my fondest childhood memories concern this annual event, not least being told where to relocate myself whilst exploring ships' sleeping quarters. As you do!

Getting in behind the deck guns and shooting down loads of enemy planes or quickly dropping the emergency life craft to escape your burning, sinking boat all fires the imagination of youth; Navy days provided the props. The trip out under the bridge (sneaking on behind the sailors' backs!) was particularly sought after. For one day we, as boys, lived the lives of men, of sailors. We lived our dreams . . superb!

Bibliography

Many and much of my reference material can be attributed to a good friend of Rosyth, Martin Rogers, and more particularly a work he was part of with Messrs. Anderson and Law "An Outline History of Rosyth Dockyard". The full text makes for essential reading for all you "ex-dockies" and is available in Rosyth Library.

Anderson, J., Rogers, M., & Law, A., (1999), "An Outline History of Rosyth Dockyard Volume 1"

Dunfermline Press, (1950), 'Rosyth Dockyard's Future - Provost Gellatly's Reassuring Statement', page 5, 4/4/1950

Dunfermline Press, (1950), 'Dockyard' Worker Suspended', page 5, 25/3/1950

Dunfermline Press, (1950), 'Letters to the Editor - Suspended Dockyard Employee: Mr. Copeland's Statement', page 4, 8/4/1950

Dunfermline Press, (1956), 'Ghost Ship of the Dockyard - Labourer's Graphic Story of Experience on HMS Glory, page 7, 7/1/1956

Dunfermline Press, (1950), 'King's Road Lighting', page 2, 11/1/1950

Dunfermline Press, (1950), 'Letters to the Editor', page 4, 18/3/1950

Rosyth during the 1980s

Martin Rogers

The 1960s and 1970s had seen an expansion in Rosyth's boundaries with new houses being built at Elder Place, Primrose and Whinnyburn. The Dollytown area had been redeveloped and, possibly linked to the opening of the Forth Road Bridge in 1964, some small business enterprises had come to Rosyth, Lyle and Scott's factory in Primrose Lane being one of the first. A number of new buildings were opened including the Methodist Church, Camdean Community Centre and the Fire Station. This had also been a time of expansion for the Dockyard with Rosyth becoming the lead Dockyard for refitting nuclear submarines. No. 1 Dock was extended, the Middle Jetty and P Jetty were constructed and the new shore establishment HMS Cochrane was commissioned. A large number of married quarters were built in the Hilton Road area. Against this background, Rosyth and the Dockyard entered the 1980s with reasons to be optimistic about the future.

In the late 1970s it had become possible for some tenants to buy their Council houses and when this scheme was extended in 1980 it led to a number of tenants in Rosyth buying their Council or Scottish Special Housing Association houses. Up to that point there had been very little privately owned housing in Rosyth but probably spurred on by the sale of the Council and SSHA houses, a number of private builders developed small estates in Rosyth in the 1980s.

Dunfermline District Council had played its part in encouraging private house ownership by selling off the former prefabs site in Camdean Crescent/Park Road (West) in the late 70s. This site was sold as a number of individual feus and a small estate of some 25 houses was created over the next few years. Rennies built the Park Lea estate in the Burnside area in 1981/82 and this was fairly quickly followed by two Robertson Homes developments - Wemyss Court in 1984 and at the Middlebank Street/Woodside Avenue corner in 1985. Walker Homes developed part of the former Dollytown area in 1986 (Granville Way) and there were developments at Mossbank in the Burnside area in 1986, at The Woodlands off Wemyss Street in 1989 and at the corner of Admiralty Road/Castle Road (also in 1989). The Royal British Legion Housing Association started work on their sheltered housing complex (Calum Macdonald Court) in 1985.

The first new house appears on the former prefabs site in Camdean, 1978
(Martin Rogers)

Considering its size, Rosyth had always been lacking in public buildings. The 1980s saw some progress in this respect with the erection of new Social Work Offices in Park Road in November 1982 closely followed by a new Health Centre in August 1983. Although there was a general welcome for these developments there were concerns about building on land which formed part of the Public Park. Would this be the thin end of the wedge leading to building development being proposed on other parts of the Public Park? Fortunately this did not happen.

The access road into the new Park Lea estate July 1981 (Martin Rogers)

The site for the new housing scheme at Granville Way in 1986
(Martin Rogers)

On the social front, the Community Festival which had started in 1978 continued successfully into the 80s. In 1982, Inverkeithing School produced a second edition of their very successful book on the "Story of Rosyth" which is still in demand today. The Adult Training Centre at Harley Street closed in March 1981 and the premises were let by Dunfermline District Council to Rosyth Rugby Club and to a Community Association. The part leased by the Community Association was used for various activities including Kung Fu, a Youth Club, a Boxing Club and a Mother and Toddlers' Group.

The site of the Social Work Offices in Park Road in 1981
The Parkgate Institute is in the background (Martin Rogers)

Local singer Carol Anders performs at the opening of the 1980 Community Festival
(Martin Rogers)

Start of a Road Race as part of the Community Festival in 1980.
The buildings of the Adult Training Centre can be seen in the background.
(Martin Rogers)

In 1980, the Clydesdale Bank extended their premises in Queensferry Road and in March of the following year the Trustees Savings Bank (formerly the Dunfermline Savings Bank) moved to the larger premises they now occupy in the Queen's Buildings. They had previously operated from small premises in Admiralty Road adjoining

Site for the new William Low's supermarket in 1981
(formerly a petrol station) (Martin Rogers)

the Police Station (now the Ex-Servicemen's Club). Another firm to go up in the world was William Low who opened a new supermarket at the north end of Queensferry Road in August 1982 (the current day Tesco store). Their former premises near Parkgate were taken over by Minor Bingo Entertainments in August 1983.

A smaller scale but nonetheless important development for the local community was the construction of new shop units in Heath Road replacing the two shops which had served the former Dollytown area. A suite of premises comprising a mini supermarket, video library, hairdressing salon and lounge bar public house (the "Glad Yer Inn") was opened at the end of 1983 by Janet and Jimmy Innes. Another Rosyth pub, the Golden Age, in Queensferry Road was re-opened in June 1985 after refurbishment and was re-named Cleos.

Two old shops in Heath Road. These were replaced by the Glad Yer Inn complex at the end of 1983 (Martin Rogers)

The Co-op movement had always been strong in Fife but in the face of increased competition from supermarkets, there was a gradual amalgamation of the various societies in order to compete. In 1980, it was the turn of Dunfermline Co-op to merge with others in Fife to form the Fife Regional Co-op Service. This led to a cost cutting programme and in 1984 the Co-op store in Camdean Lane was closed to be followed in 1889 by the closure of the Discount Centre at the top of Backmarch Road.

Dunfermline Co-op Store in Camdean Lane shortly before its closure in 1984
(Martin Rogers)

In the mid 1980s, Dunfermline District Council designated the original Garden City part of Rosyth as a Conservation Area with the aim of preserving the character of the area. By that time a number of tenants had bought their houses and were seeking to replace windows and doors, harl the walls and add conservatories, porches and the like. At about the same time, the SSHA embarked on a programme of improvements to their older housing stock in Rosyth designed to upgrade the interiors and improve the appearance of the houses themselves (new doors, colour washing the exteriors). Unfortunately the schemes to colour wash the houses in different colours could not be fully implemented as a number of the houses had been sold and the result was a generally unsatisfactory patchwork of bright colours in pink, yellow and orange with the original brown colour and new harling interspersed.

The Conservation Area designation soon came under criticism as the owners of properties found that they were unable to alter their properties in the way they wanted. In a referendum held in 1989 among the residents in the designated area, a significant majority of those voting favoured the withdrawal of the Conservation Area status. Sadly, in my view, the District Council bowed to this expression of public opinion and removed the designation in 1990. The result has been a loss of the character of the Garden City. Two familiar landmarks disappeared in the mid 1980s. In 1984 the former School Meals Kitchen in Fairykirk Road was demolished. This had been built in the mid 1940s but had become redundant when it was decided to provide kitchen facilities at each school. In November 1986, the St. Andrew and St. George Scottish Episcopal Church was demolished. This Church had been established in Rosyth in 1917, meeting initially in a wooden hut at the Crossroads. Their permanent Church building, designed by architect Sir Ninian Comper, was opened in January 1926 and, at the time of its demolition, was one of the few listed buildings in Rosyth. A small housing development (Mellor Court) was built on the site.

The former School Meals Kitchen in Fairykirk Road in 1974 (Martin Rogers)

St. Andrew & St. George Scottish Episcopal Church in 1986 shortly
before its demolition (Martin Rogers)

Later in the decade (1988) the long awaited new Rosyth Library was opened on a site in the public park close to Parkgate Community Centre to be followed shortly afterwards by the new St. John's RC Primary School in Heath Road. The former school site in Crossroads Place was developed for housing by the Margaret Blackwood Housing Association, mainly intended for disabled and older people. A police call point was also established.

St. John's RC Primary School opened in 1988
(Martin Rogers)

For the Dockyard and Naval Base, the 1980s was a decade of mixed fortunes. An important new development at the beginning of the decade was the syncrolift complex which was brought into use in October 1980. This allowed smaller vessels to be lifted out of the water and taken into covered accommodation for repairs and refits. HMS Gavinton, a mine countermeasures vessel, was the first to be refitted in the syncrolift complex. By January 1983, 100 vessels had been docked in this way.

HMS Gavinton being taken into the Syncrolift Complex in October 1980
(Dunfermline Carnegie Library - Morris Allan Collection)

The Nott Defence Review in 1981 resulted in the closure of Gibraltar and Chatham Dockyards and the reduction of Portsmouth Dockyard to Fleet Maintenance status. Rosyth gained from these closures with additional work coming to Rosyth which would otherwise have been carried out at Chatham. Another additional and unexpected workload came in 1982 when the Dockyard was heavily involved in preparing ships for the South Atlantic Task Force during the Falklands War.

HMS Plymouth returning from the Falklands War to a rousing welcome
(Dunfermline Carnegie Library)

HMS Abdiel in floating Dock AFD 26 circa 1987 (Babcock)

With the opening of the Syncrolift in 1980, the last remaining floating dock (AFD 22) had been removed from Rosyth. However, as a result of an increasing workload, floating dock AFD 26 was brought up from Portsmouth in 1984.

In 1985 Rosyth became the home base for four of the new Type 42 Destroyers, HM Ships Edinburgh, Glasgow, York and Liverpool and a new Tango Berth and Lowden Accommodation Block were built for this purpose. A new Police Station (the McMillan Building) was built at the Dockyard gates and was opened in November 1985 and the following February a new West Access Road was built. At this time, about 9000 civilian and 3000 naval personnel were working or based at Rosyth. It was not all good news, however, as the Royal Naval Engineering School, HMS Caledonia, closed at the end of 1985. This was a sad occasion as the establishment had been at Rosyth since 1937 and during this time many local girls had found sweethearts and husbands from among the ranks of the "tiffs". The complex of buildings became part of HMS Cochrane.

Gate of the Royal Naval Engineering School (HMS Caledonia) in 1978
(Martin Rogers)

Perhaps the most significant and controversial event of the decade so far as the Dockyard was concerned was the introduction of commercial management. After a bidding process, Babcock Thorn took over the running of the Dockyard for a seven year period from April 1987. There was general opposition to this move but being under commercial management did allow the Dockyard to use the skills of the work force in other areas. Within four or five years this work accounted for about 10% of the total workload.

HMS Churchill arriving at Rosyth for a refit in 1989. About half way through the refit it was cancelled because of defence cuts and the submarine was de-commissioned. St. Margaret's Hope, the official residence of the Flag Officer Scotland, Northern England and Northern Ireland, can be seen in the background. (Babcock)

So how to sum up the effect of the 1980s on Rosyth and the Dockyard? For some years previously, Rosyth had steadily been moving away from the position of a Dockyard Town where the majority of the working population were employed in the Dockyard. There had once been a regular movement of families to and from the southern dockyards and to Dockyards overseas. This had reduced in the 1970s and more so in the 1980s as Dockyards were closed and those which were left came under commercial management. The housing estates built in Rosyth in the 1950s, 60s and 70s were not specifically for Dockyard workers. Taken together with the sale of Council and SSHA houses and the building of private housing estates in the 1980s, the population of Rosyth became less and less dependent on the Dockyard for employment.

So far as the Dockyard was concerned, there was apprehension about the effects of commercial management and whether this would eventually lead to privatisation of the Dockyard. At the beginning of 1990, the Government's 'Options for Change', following the end of the Cold War, proposed significant cuts in the size of the nuclear submarine fleet and of surface ships. However, the fact that the Dockyard had been chosen to refit the new class of Trident submarines seemed to guarantee its future for many years to come albeit on a reduced scale. Sadly the 1990s was to have some unpleasant surprises in store for the Dockyard and Naval Base although the town of Rosyth continued to benefit from new businesses coming into the area.

Bibliography

"An Outline History of Rosyth Dockyard", (1999), Jack Anderson, Martin Rogers and Alex Law. Prepared as part of the Carnegie Dunfermline Trust's 20th Century Dunfermline Project - held in the Local History Department of Dunfermline Carnegie Library

Rosyth in the 21st Century

Margaret Shiach

This chapter is dedicated to the memory of Pamela Iris Blair (1922-2004), a true friend to the people, animals and wild birds of Rosyth.

In 1995 Rosyth ceased to be a Naval Base and the ships of the 1st and 3rd Mine Countermeasure Squadrons and the Fishery Protection Squadron moved to Faslane and Portsmouth. This was yet another blow to the Dockyard, following on the decisions in the early 1990s to reduce the size of the Royal Navy after the end of the Cold War and, in 1993, that Devonport would refit the Trident submarines. The Trident decision cast a long shadow over the future of the Dockyard as the programme of allocated ship refit work announced at that time would come to an end in 2007.

Lexmark, Admiralty Park, Rosyth
(Lexmark International (Scotland) Ltd.)

It was not all doom and gloom, however, with Babcock Rosyth Ltd., the owners of the Dockyard, having diversified their operations to attract other business. New industrial and commercial companies had been attracted to the Rosyth area with the Dunfermline Building Society and BSkyB opening premises in the Carnegie Campus in 1994 and 1995 respectively. In 1996 the US based international company Lexmark opened new premises on the former Fleet Grounds in Admiralty Road creating around 500 jobs. Lexmark are manufacturers and worldwide suppliers of printers and ink cartridges for the computing industry. The company has flourished and is a main employer in the area.

Rosyth in the 21st Century is a thriving community: the rise has begun. The projected 2004 Government population figures for Rosyth is approximately 12,500. Over 60% of the population is of employable age and many travel by car, bus and train outwith Rosyth to work in areas such as Dunfermline and Edinburgh. This is not because there are no opportunities for employment in Rosyth - far from it!

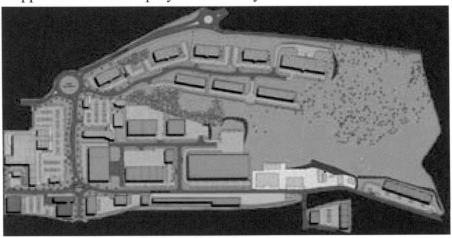

Plan of Rosyth Europark
(Innovation http//www.rebic.co.uk)

Today, Rosyth can boast of a huge variety of employers. In addition to the local small businesses such as newsagents, chemists, **a** health centre, two doctor's surgeries, butchers, several bakers and post offices, at the backbone of the community, there are also the bigger employers, such as the banks and supermarkets. Rosyth is not only home to these but to timber, electrical and engineering firms and to businesses offering employment in communications, graphics and computing.

Rosyth Europarc Business Innovation Centre
(Innovation http//www.rebic.co.uk)

Intelligent Finance Offices, March 2004

Rosyth is rejuvenating the Naval Base area. Rosyth Europarc, backed by Scottish Enterprise Fife and the European Regional Development Fund, opened in October 2000, at a cost of £10 million for the infrastructure upgrade, and a further £12.25 million was invested in their new-build programme. It is housed on part of the site of the former HMS Cochrane and has enough space for 15 businesses. One of these businesses is VeriSIM, being a suppler of innovative web technology solutions to UK customers.

Also based here is The Royal Bank Of Scotland and Intelligent Finance. A new concept in banking, Intelligent Banking, is web based and is the result of a merging of the Bank of Scotland and Halifax Plc. The company put down roots in Rosyth Europarc and was officially opened in 2002. Since then it has become one of the country's leading direct banking companies.

(Photos Courtesy of Lauder College)

Rosyth is looking to the future and tackling it head on. In October 2000, Babcock Engineering Services and Lauder College joined forces to revolutionise engineering training in the East of Scotland.

This is a 'unique concept' to the East of Scotland – an engineering firm and an educational institution joining together to make changes. It gives employers in technology and related areas a focal point, providing information about access to first class training. Students can receive 'Modern Apprenticeships' and those looking to improve their qualifications can join 'up-skilling programmes' whereby the training is designed to meet the needs of the individual.

The Port of Rosyth was established in 1997 by Forth Ports Authority and in 1999 gained more land which extended it to around 100 acres. The port provides the operating base for commercial operations with such raw materials as coal and timber being landed there. It is also the docking area for cruise liners as well as the base for Superfast's ferry service. In 2001, the Ports Authority were given a £12 million award from the Government, '... the biggest maritime grant ever awarded' to work with Superfast to provide a link to mainland Europe. *(Evening News, 2001)* Superfast launched their ferry service in Rosyth on 17 May 2002, opening up the area with a direct link to mainland Zeebrugge, Belgium.

Superfast Ferry beneath Forth Rail Bridge
(J7 Digital Photography: www.jseven.co.uk)

Rosyth now boasts a magnificent Ferry Terminal Building, which was officially opened by Chancellor of the Exchequer Gordon Brown on 23 May 2003 to 'celebrate' the end of the first year of operation for Superfast's Rosyth to Zeebrugge service.

Rosyth's new Ferry Terminal

With the ferry services has come the potential to turn Rosyth into an international gateway, Europe being only an overnight sail away. The service carried some 300,000 passengers for the year February 2003-2004. The ferry is also very popular with haulage firms – three hundred are now using the service, making it a highly sought after mode of transporting goods from Scotland to mainland Europe. By May 2004, it established haulage links to the newly joined EU country, Slovenia. *(Evening News, 2004)*

Although there is no longer any submarine work done in her docks, in 2003/2004, Rosyth saw the aircraft carriers HMS Ark Royal and HMS Invincible gracing the Forth whilst being refitted. In 2004 Babcock Engineering Services completed a £117 million refit of HMS Illustrious.

The only Royal Naval facility that remains in the area is HMS Caledonia which provides the support needed for stand-by naval personnel from the ships currently undergoing refit.

In the late 1990s the Ministry of Defence started to sell off various areas for development and a large proportion of their housing stock. These houses were snapped up quickly and the area is now fully occupied by either private owners or private tenants. There are, however, some houses in the area that are still owned by the MOD, for example those in Ferrytoll Place.

Two major building companies have recently developed some of the residential sites. The houses are modern and are quickly bought by families wishing to move into the area. There are a large number of families moving to Rosyth from Edinburgh since house prices in Edinburgh are out of reach of many starting a family. Rosyth is a convenient commuter area as a result of its rail and road links to Edinburgh over the Forth Road and Rail Bridges.

Persimmon have built in the area formerly known as Pease Hill. They have built both houses and flats, with more building work expected to continue for quite some time. Wimpey are also building homes in the area at Forth View, just off Hilton Road.

Pease Hill Road in Persimmon Homes – Admiral Heights Development
(Martin Rogers)

New flats at Admiral Heights

Completed Homes at the Wimpey Site at Forth View

Cochranes Hotel
(Martin Rogers)

Watson House, a former dockyard hostel, in Hilton Road has now been developed to become Cochrane's Hotel, which opened as a fully operating hotel at the end of 2002. Also nearby, St. Margaret's Church has been developed to become The Sub Station, a recording studio that provides engineers, equipment and advice to both up-and-coming and well-established artists from the Drifters, Nazareth, Big Country and Texas to Mogwai, Rancid and Elastica.

The Sub Station Recording Studio
(Martin \Rogers)

Many of the houses in the original Garden City area are under private ownership and the facings of these houses are now greatly varied.

Many of the roads around these areas also now have speed bumps. These are a bit of a mixed blessing; they have certainly slowed down traffic in the area. Whilst the local residents understand the need for them, like others up and down the country, many do not like them. One recent comment was that they created a nautical, sea-rolling effect as you drove over them, in keeping with the naval theme of the area – or in reality, that they made one child feel sea sick in the car!

The doctors' surgery in Queensferry Road has moved to a new purpose built Health Centre in Primrose Lane. The old surgery buildings in Queensferry Road were bought by Leonard Cheshire Homes and, in July 2002, they opened a day centre for disabled young adults. This establishment provides care for those with physical disabilities, learning difficulties and those who need respite care and rehabilitation.

Primrose Lane Surgery

The new surgery has been built beside the complex that was known until recently as the Leisure Zone. In the 90s it housed a bowling alley which has unfortunately now closed due to financial difficulties. Part of the building is still used as a keep-fit centre.

Although Rosyth is looking to the future, it is not without some concern for the area. The result of Rosyth's expansion, both in industry and housing, has created new worries. Rosyth is in danger of merging with neighbouring Dunfermline, the tree lined walk ways in Primrose Lane are gone and there is concern, like many areas country-wide, over Rosyth's wild bird population. In the past yellowhammers, skylarks and herons have all been seen in this area. The fear now is that their numbers will be in decline if more scrubland is used for new building. The area's appearance is changing; the original concept of housing interspersed with green spaces is gradually being eroded away.

King's Road School
(Martin Rogers)

In 2001, King's Road Primary School was set on fire and unfortunately had to be demolished. A state of the art, new, energy-saving Primary school now stands in its place. The building itself is a hugely motivating experience for those who pass through its doors to learn. For some, the building of the new King's Road School has caused concern that the appearance of this very modern building in the area is adding to the erosion of the heritage of the area. The question is should Rosyth's modern housing and industrial success be accomplished at the expense of a wonderful heritage and architectural achievement? A balance has to be found, since without embracing of new ideas and concepts, Rosyth would not have been created in the first instance. Yet to lose its wonderful heritage would be a grave loss to the future generations of Rosyth.

Many people have passed through Rosyth over the years, each with their own lasting memories. Those who have stayed and whose families have stayed have their own stories to tell. In writing this book, we want to invest in Rosyth's future generations. The most precious things we have in our society today are its children. It is through the children who grow up here that Rosyth will either continue to grow and flourish or decline. I believe that children should learn from their own local history and take ownership in their own communities. Adults need to reinforce the unique history of Rosyth and show respect for it. It is by example that children will either learn to work with their local communities or against them. I hope that by writing this book, we have played a small part in enabling Rosyth to claim its unique and rightful place in Scottish history.

Bibliography

Population statistics courtesy of General Register office for Scotland, Ladywell House, Ladywell Road, Edinburgh

Evening News, 2001, *£12m handout secures Rosyth ferry plan* , article id 1501782001, [on-line] available from: http://news.scotsman.com/archive.

Evening News, 2004, *Rosyth ferry to run freight link to new EU country*, article id 57167, [on-line] available from: http://news.scotsman.com/archive.

Lexmark, 2004, *About us*, [on-line] available from: http://www.lexmark.com

Forth Ports Authority, 2004, Corporate Information (History), [on-line] available from: http://ww7.investorrelations.co.uk/forthports/corporate/history.jsp

The Sub Station, 2004, Client, [on-line] available from: http://members.madasafish. com/%7Esub station/subWeb.htm (Sub Station Recording Studio)

The International Council on Monuments and Sites

The International Council on Monuments and Sites, (ICOMOS), is an international, non-governmental organisation dedicated to the conservation of the world's historic monuments and sites. The organisation was founded in 1965, and has national committees in 107 countries all over the world. ICOMOS is UNESCO's principal advisor in matters concerning the conservation and protection of monuments and sites. UNESCO – the United Nations Educational, Scientific and Cultural Organisation – was established on 16 November 1945. Today, UNESCO promotes international co-operation between its 190 member and six associate members in the fields of education, science, culture and communication. Through its International Scientific Committees around the world, ICOMOS endeavours to set standards for 'preservation, restoration, and management of the cultural environment.' *(ICOMOS, 2004)*.

ICOMOS's findings on Garden Cities, and on Rosyth in particular

'The great, designed, social housing schemes, built initially in response to changing social and industrial pressures from the growth of the industrial cities of the UK at the turn of the 19th/20th century, are now beginning to attract much interest as a UK phenomenon. At the same time, their overall designs are becoming vulnerable to fragmentation as individual choices work against the significance of their whole concepts.

By degrees, the Garden City concept, which involved designs for the spatial organisation of people as well as for individual commercial and domestic buildings, evolved into Garden Suburbs, where housing predominated and the design concepts were centred on the layout of roads, houses and open spaces.

The risks that particularly affect garden cities and suburbs come not from demolition or lack of use, but rather from the slow but persistent erosion of the overall coherence that typified their initial designs. These creeping threats result from the impact of new economic developments, from inadequate planning controls to stop changes to details and from application of such elements as traffic calming measures – which generate a mass of signs and other devices that often do not respect the special character of an area. Conservation areas have been designated in some garden suburbs, but the majority remain vulnerable to fragmentation and loss of identity.' *(ICOMOS, 2004)*

Rosyth Garden City, Fife

This garden city, at the end of the Forth Bridge, was designed by AM Mottram and built in 1916 by the Admiralty for workers at the Rosyth Docks. It illustrates the top end of a fragmentation process, with many houses being sold to private individuals and with no conservation area to maintain the consistency of character of the houses. The result is a sad loss of coherence and character.'

(ICOMOS, 2004)

Bibliography

Denyer, S. & Cresswell, E., 2002, United Kingdom 20th Century Heritage at Risk (Rosyth Garden City, Fife), [on-line] available from: http://www.international.icomos.org/risk/2002/uk2002.htm

Financial Support

This book would not have been possible without the very generous support of the following organisations:

Royal Incorporation of Architects in Scotland - funded by the Royal Incorporation of Architects in Scotland Millennium Awards

  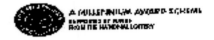

Millennium Awards

A MILLENNIUM AWARD SCHEME SUPPORTED BY FUNDS FROM THE NATIONAL LOTTERY

Canvas Holidays Ltd.

Fife Council Locality Group

Fife Council Education Department

Teesdale & Muir Homes (Scarborough Holdings)

Tullis Russell Papermakers